LIMBINAL

LIMBINAL

WITH TRANSLATIONS OF PAUL CELAN

Oana Avasilichioaei

TALONBOOKS

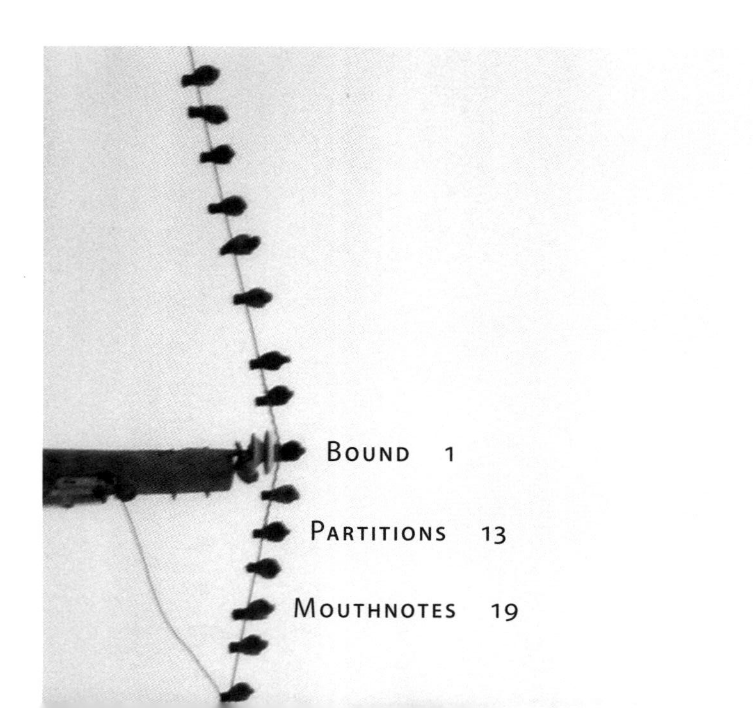

Bound 1

Partitions 13

Mouthnotes 19

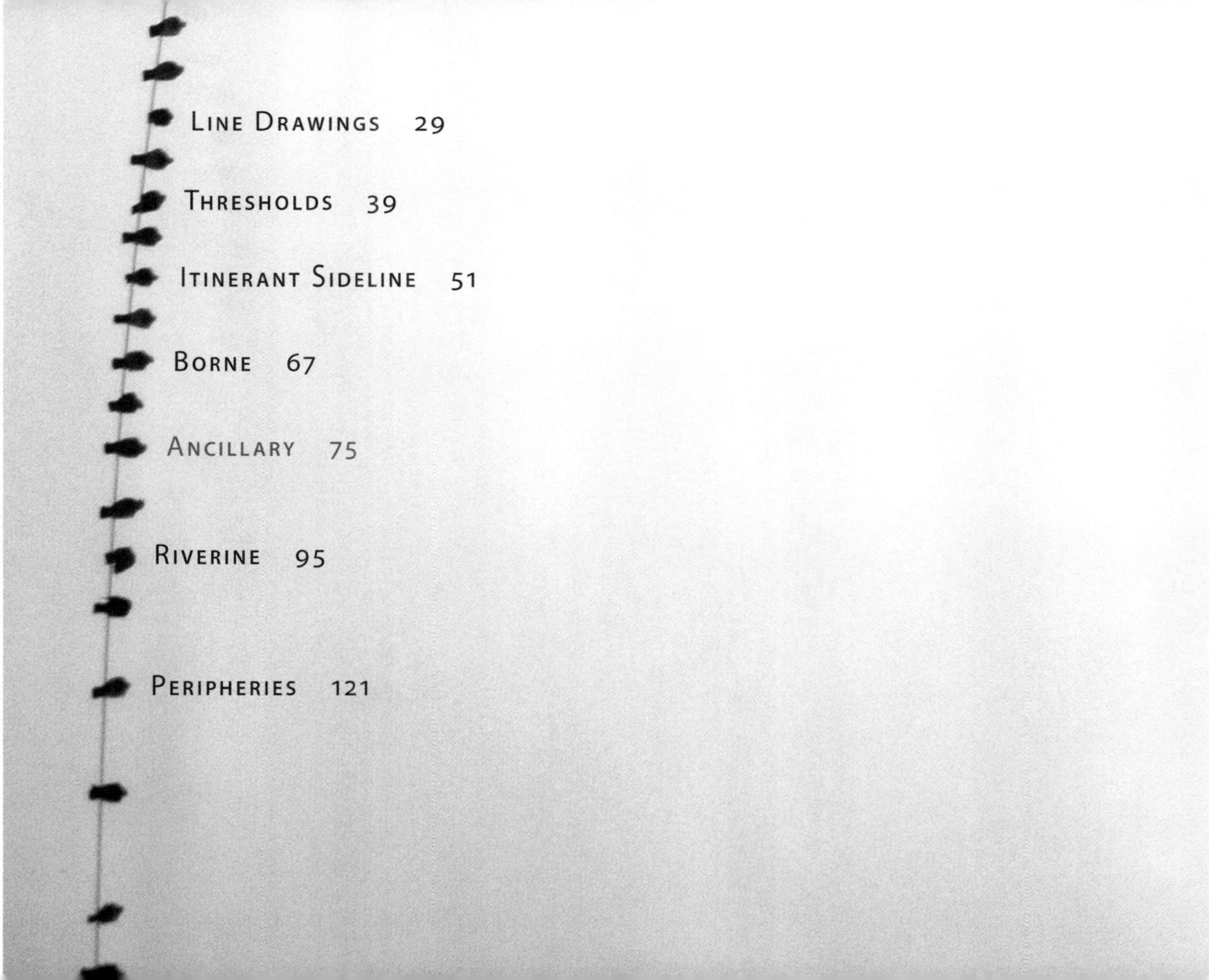

Line Drawings 29

Thresholds 39

Itinerant Sideline 51

Borne 67

Ancillary 75

Riverine 95

Peripheries 121

Bound

Border, you terrify. Border, you must dictate your own dismantling or we will perish. Purge. Border, are you listening? Are you empire?

The geography keeps shifting into bloom and decay, thus daring to future. Periphery disrupts the dialogue. Floundering, wet lines linger. Fish bend the river into its undulations, spring curves. Will these trajectories double back, mislead us? We leave unnoticed through a back gate to make a country elsewhere. We pass the perennials and smile softly. What is our spatialized intention?

Our margin is a pinprick. One of us balances. We enter the idea sideways, disjunctive, producing architectures, performing language, inscribing intervals. The city rumbles into a future because it lacks direction. Frequencies jam. Then our distortions wander. How do we chart this aliveness? Of marginal weathers, of limited instruction, passage inserts here.

Perhaps a meridian is what we look for. If you insist that I take sides, you will misplace me. Instead, I take a barrier to the woods and grow confusion, which might be a sign of health, though a leader does not think so.

Border, walking along your edges, I realize that what from a distance appears as edge is simply a faded memory. The moment unravels around us, thought-struck. Border, as an idea, you are impossible to margin. Border, are you listening? Are you hungry? Still hoping for empire?

We vacate the bedroom. We are an outskirt in disguise. We serrate sounding. Sink. Tending to a voice is tending to a throat. In thinking of a tender her, contours ripple. On the eve of the departure, hands are already parched, mouth is already empty.

Border, are you watching? Your scope tuned towards an obscure gesture, your gaze indifferent. While a rippling refrain of shots, tasers, accelerated feet and sleepless hands rages. Border, are you enraged? Are you bored? Are you longing for the fiction of enlightenment?

Daytime obstructs our watching, though we remain vigilant. Our watching, itself a dismantling of boundary. Stutter, cough into. Caught. It's not about being on one side or the other, but about one side being the other. Border, are you nervous? Nerves? Nodes? Are you a call to network?

To cross the island of the self to the island of another. Because she shows me how. Border, does this incite you? Does your shore lust for another's shore? When the other encroaches and thus smalls the self. When the other inspires and thus expands the self. Land of transpresence. Awake.

In defecting from the I's island, its shored nationhood, my I still rations I to I. Hybrid as a space of doubt. Or manufactured hope for future. Resistance in being. Being in resistance. In these words, histories unfold. Impossible to utter without attachments clamouring at the mouth. No word is a virgin. Hybrood. Nationmood. Or is it? Immigraftion. Immiration.

Border, are you minding the native in us? Are you pining for home? So easily lost to distraction, fear grips. In the territory of a being, territory accumulates. Occult incision. We grasp nomadic, supplicants at the thresholds to our own selves.

The child ushered by officious adults across a windowsill to wave the nation's flag (rectangle of coloured paper glued to a short stick) among a school of flagging children. Teachers or patriotic composers conduct the young symphony of adulation. Years stand on the terrace of the "people's palace."

Ache in child hands, spectacle of orchestrated colour. Unnatural sea of cheer, perfectly coordinated tides. Organic mechanism will-stripped yet surviving. From the windowsill with the child, a wish to defect, yet will not or cannot.

Ostensibly, an I can and does become a commodity. My I accommodates. And they wondered about our aversion to demonstrations. Yet we manifest masses as a feeling body, not a thinking body. Responsive and responsible only if autonomous. Border, you will us to stop thinking yet we.

Hands washed clean to discolouration. Or the desire to. Though wanting it so doesn't make it so. In the puddle's humble reflection of sky, a presence. Will the weeping begin? Such is a self confining itself in language.

Edge divulges an entrance. A sign obstructs the view. We need a sunset to see the horizon or the horizon to compose a sunset. Condos are blossoming and we are careful. A map spreads out for us to invent over and over again.

Between our contours the edifice becoming. Contours engaged in touching, teasing out transparent flux of envelope. Breathe, there, in the room of our chest cavity. Is our limb your corridor? Limber door? Core?

Border, are you primitive? Are you primed for capital, economics, policy? The child, pointless sandwich in hand, spends lunch hour circling the school building. No one dares the outside to befriend her foreignness. Nuclear threat once more in the schoolyard of leaders.

A breathing tree, a strewn sentence, a mundane alley of cement. We veer to have nothing to say yet stubborn until the saying comes. Juncture as meeting point and phonetic feature for distinguishing a word's boundary.

The child wades into the river, curious for the other side, daring the farther of one shore, the closer of the other. The child loses footing, gulps, flounders in the current. Time distills, panics into rushing limbs, flailing water, gasps for air, water, water. Then a stranger's strong arms, air carried ashore. Border, are we collecting your confinements?

Border, in principle, we reject your unprincipled discipline, your corrupt yoke. In action, we are immobile, static, ineffectual. Not quite ashamed enough to act. As such, words become unsanitary, a choreographed arrangement of marks on screen or paper. Born virtual to expire virtual. Virtuous, an obsolete. Border, now you see how easy it is to extricate yourself from our facade.

Within the bounds of a body, a scrambling network, anachronistic village, virtual sky, a physical location in a dislocation, a here in a there, a there in a here, her languages in my languages, my languages in his, urbanized seagulls, brick, glass, corrugated skylines.

Border, do we tease you with our marginalia? Theatrical animal space. Broken planks of laughter. Boards. Earnestness mistaken for emphatic surrender. When in mildness, a sky betrays plumes of travel and decline.

Solitudes in a new arrangement. The frontier question being whether or not I will enter the other side's economy. Urged to declare my participation. Anxiety that I won't. Alien body as fiscal threat. Should I mention that my frequent crossing is propelled by love not market?

We wanted to theorize the voice, give it credence in the angle of an article. A rumour's embroilment, its flimsy insistence, floating there, obnoxiously, perversely real. This is no precipice or chasm but full fear. At this crossing, an anecdote would be useful but (in today's margin) we lack such colour.

We are exalted and broken. Search for the day's voice. Grope, claw, paw, finger, scratch, ink, tap. Skin bears a melodious scent. I am my fear and my fear's sworn enemy. Glare at the scarred, burdened words of discord. Uncontainable. In the face of such thisness, how can the matter of any language matter? How can it not?

Border, are you mocking with your burden of media? Your well-informed mediocrity? Profanely studded highways stacking notches on your seductive belt. You scan, x ray, print, declare a full picture, a digital dissection of a body. Belonging, in your barrier, to a state and to a subject.

To manifest dissent and lumber danger. In woods, plains, gorges we trigger softly, while a leader calmly drinks a morning's conflict. Border of surveillance, I anticipate your cringing. Avert. Trench in. Like a suggestive glance. Supple curve of her ribs.

I as polyphonous composition or polygamous sound key. A folding of the self into the self of the self. Resonance of her hand against my hip. Lunge. Linger. Provisional yet recurrent. Rebellious. Before our eyes, the frontier growing into an industry of identifiers, their torment. Here we might forage for the means to our own handling.

The child feels along a balustrade of impenetrable darkness. Terrified, yet penetrating. The condition is that she must reach the skylight, its stairwell. A sisyphean task she burrows daily in her ration of apple. The condition is that there are always conditions. Some more bitter than others.

Planting our legs firmly on the ground, which is to say splitting our I's into two stillnesses, we sneak-preview a defiant stance, which is to say we politick in standing so politics elude us, which is to say that our projection is slack in sense and possibly repetitive, which is to say that our defiance is immobile. Allegedly, a new leader succeeds a leader trying to prove the sense of *leader*.

Border, like a mime, groupie, devout follower, congregation member, fan, I keep trying to become my own institution. Though seemingly unfettered, daily I sit at a desk and institutionalize.

Border, are you moving for your own comfort? Indignant? Fickle with unease? As you mount your narcissusean reflection. Aggress for battle. As though between an ever-present enemy. We spring gregarious in our innocence. Or ignorance. Cross the ramshackle footbridge of empty space and rotting boards. Border, are you sexless in your own metonymy? Yet aim your loaded metaphors in our directions?

In the screaming letter, we unwittingly mingle. Noise stationing us. Pinned. Territorial? How this word stalks and preys. How years are celled not on *home soil*. Lives kept breathing, though not living.

In broaching our own margins, we homage. Border, you loom on the horizon, or the limit of perception, an unruly spectre. We blink sideways and roar. Mobilize. Thirst. In the void, her tongue a sudden catalyst. I still. In spacious wonderment.

The building blushes a crinoline of people, line of empty hands hopeful for lilies or orchids. Or some other pastime like gelato. The pale delicacy of her wrist. Tendering from social surplus to pulsing ardour, I pervert. Border, you keep straying us into a former century. Some days we can resist, some days we cannot.

Our vocation is to meta or to muster the material. Vocalize our vocatives. Visceral and voracious. I have been called thus. Yet at times I fail to conference a new confluence of meaning. Border, do not vilify our rigour, though we tempt you.

The child takes dictation of words she can't identify, yet whose forms she tries to render. The first random words that grow to meaning, *horse* and *factory*, are encountered in the child's body as revelatory entrances into the new idiom. Body transforming through the new language. Language transforming through the new body. A hoofed neigh with moist eyes and slick shape emerges from the wall of sound, then an assembled rumble of smoke and steel concretizes in the reforming field of vision. And the child grasps that the wall of sound can and will become *language*.

We re-enter the bedroom to reinvent our borders. Unbound. The rhythmic of our worded throbbing. Handling of our geographical. Reclining on the unmade bed, the city spreads vistas before us. We brood, brooding on the threshold, listening for a hinge to unhinge us.

Partitions

Mouthtuned

Lipped lunge of language cavities
In particular his human tongue
Handkerchiefs into mouths
From the dead man's mouth
False prophecies voiced leaves
Bites belated from my language brow
A maybe's warning foliage
To be told what awaits chokes tomorrow
Eaten with memory's spoon
Into a glass in one single gloss silence unfreezes
Voice wills to announce
Monosyllabic courageous acts
Will I swallow murmurful goblets?
Speak wildly blaze
Waters drunk from the silenced?
Throng sigh say again
Glut the table of poisons with our reawakened laughter?
Until his dreaming tongue
Incestuously kiss my own honeyed tongue?
Our found common tongue mouths a name
In particular his human tongue
Lipped lunge of language cavities
From the dead man's mouth
Handkerchiefs into mouths
To be told what awaits chokes tomorrow
False prophesies voiced leaves
Into a glass in one single gloss silence unfreezes
A maybe's warning foliage
Voice wills to announce
Eaten with memory's spoon
Speak wildly blaze
Monosyllabic courageous acts
Will I swallow murmurful goblets?
Throng sigh say again
Waters drunk from the silenced?
Until his dreaming tongue
Glut the table of poisons with our reawakened laughter?
Our found common tongue mouths a name
Incestuously kiss my own honeyed tongue?

Browshore

on your brow, morning wakes cross-eyed
sky, an argument where the owned
dispute over their crown of scales
tattooing the budding hour in the skin
of your temples unsettled and greedy to clamour
inside your helmet, bite from your brow
which is a casement, a wreathed summit,
a drifting vault, reach this shore of yourself
slabs of lids rise, as though from a temple
where a leaf settles, then mounts to the swollen sky,
the window, where we scramble as though to a shelter
to watch, slumberous and dishevelled, the sky
bear down on your laurel-adorned temple, eyes' hoods
contour of these dew-torn thoughts, an island?
a mirage? a splintered profile?

Dishevelled Helmet

hair streaming
from trees   from hands,
twilight-sown,   from mirrors
slumbering hair   foliage forever dishevelled
cascades burst through
the shadowed swamp,
after all   frozen lake
the fruitless
curtains of tresses   waiting
trace   voice courageous
hair's shadow   in the breeze
feather   in the sand
the somnolent sky   of a palm
halo of an aerial   to dusk
shipwreck   with your raven
dishevel me up the stairs
await, spectacular
to dissemble   in your mane,
my curtain,   on the final step
endless   my hooded,
ramifications of   my exile
my   aerial roots
concrescent
shimmering   heady prophecy
in tresses of uncertainties
its shadow
in the sky
of your own
contradictory
word
hanging
from your throat

Shouldering

we'll slowly unfasten incessant roots, wind, foliage
sprout on our shoulders where the slow can't take root

skirmish of the great azure boulevards
if i stir depends on you

luminous shoulders, silent and with gestures, flaunt the incessant
a despair similar, where is the firmament?

if tonight i summon you will the season be hourless?
if i shoulder your season's nights will the hourless summon?

though lacking a handrail, i flood the house with spectacular
    pleasure
hand pointing to yesterday's hour, embracing all hours, a time
    much larger, heightitude, ramifications

offer my shoulder, translucent with this exploratory season
waves flood, sleeves hoist, scramble up a bloom, sprout a
    shoulder scorched

a leafed wing rambles hearing your answer
the only constellation gashing at dawn

Mouthnotes[1]

1 Yet the ouster is muzzled, the whistleblower is muzzled, the revolutionary is muzzled, the teetotaller is muzzled, the law-abiding citizen is muzzled, the rebel is muzzled, the informer is muzzled, the abstainer is muzzled, the dabbler is muzzled, the foreigner is muzzled, the conscientious objector is muzzled, the analyst is muzzled, the reformer is muzzled, the soldier is muzzled, the activist is muzzled, the volunteer is muzzled, and the muzzle is elected (or not), gun-wielding (or violent-ready) and ubiquitous.

what if resonance vocally sits in the mouth? or rather what if you vocally resonate[2] in my mouth?

---

2 we made us wet supine in the pond we tuft
woodswollen mossheavy with gesture
margin the bushy aftermath of

we wet our pines and made us swollen
often the undergrowth   often piercing through
here we might insert

we swell our made and pond us wet
in the fibrous ligature
motion joint branch stamen frond

we slick lapping between the wooded wet
jugular juncture
joining of a singular to a singular

does the mouth practise its conclusions? the sonata of linguistic ruination interrupted, shifting (sprouting)[3] in the encounter with your word, i.e., your being?

---

3 the simplicity of *a hunger in my mouth*

or *all night your hand slept on my hip bone*

to wander in the melee of matter

how *you* could feel so tender in *my* throat

the thinking house of the mouth (à la Leblanc) dwells in the angles of its recesses (lexical necessity) as prepositions commit (dive off) cliff's (mouth's) oblige[4]

---

4 the barbarians are gathering, glutting the streets, the firewires, cellular signals, anticipating a gluttonous feast

we pack in, a calamity in their wake
though we must teem
we need not mud thin confuse

how[5] to disarticulate in order to articulate?

---

5 what of truth then?
what accord to the chords?

we strew a sentence along a limb's passage
deceived into believing
we've accomplished something

inflection crease shade pleat variation tangent fluctuation hinge[6]
deviation

---

6 how a life gets living making *i*'s like furrows (tracks)

labyrinthine lab of wordmatter

bending word to fjord (fluctuate) its subject

animal pleats of oscillating dermis

vibrating intimacy of (fluid) i to (fluent) eye

you the boldest pronoun *i* pronounces

in the body's warren a face (soaring swarm) proposing[7] what angle?

---

7 in turning, the face faces with its innumerable subjects
in subjecting the turn with its faces, an i facets

faceted i slips (slopes)
                              the saying face
                                                      flips its subjects
animal face   i invents a face
notional facet   a face invents its i
speculative facet   the invention is subjective

my written mouths[8] the book and follows the book (à la Jabès)

---

8 before a word a being (an *i* perhaps)
intersects naked about
to distend into disgorging

after a word naked intersections (possibly interdictions)
traject outwards
dispersing and coalescing

while my own barbarian world
sticks in the throat
contorted into inexpression

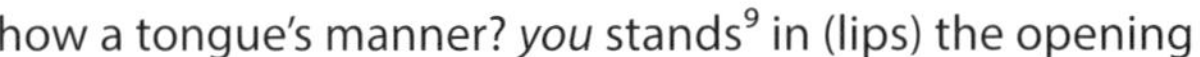

how a tongue’s manner? *you* stands[9] in (lips) the opening

---

9 stance of minding in nature
stance of meddling in notion

enveloping (vowelling) your consonant
my voice timbres

Line Drawings

The lines were drawn without our consent. This is an empty statement, for the drawing of the lines did not require our consent. We shored the river but turned away when we realized our subjectivities were seeping into it. We fought unfairly. Overgrown like wedges of land covered in weeds. With our jugular appendages, we intoned coarse sounds. Ventured to look past our moss-ridden thighs. Mostly, our soundings were futile, husked. But there were moments of lucidity, even resonance. Then our hands would reach out to touch each other's throats as though in recognition. Or acknowledgement. Petals of thought blew gusts around us. Small creatures guarded our solitudes. Which churned in the cavern of our guts. The vastness of our intention was a material we could not fathom. We asked questions that had no answers and as such perpetuated into quarries of language.

The city gates closed before we could enter. Or they had been torn down, erased. When we could not find them, we entered the city from above or backwards or backtracked to our last point of departure. Which we soon forgot. And backtracked into a corner. Upon arrival, we clothed ourselves in the same series of movements, got our bearings by walking habitual patterns into the surroundings, rearranged the furniture in the estranged rooms, made eye contact with the locals, froze a few frames of architecture and flora on our viewfinders, slept fitful nights. The city being distant, and as some act was needed to provoke momentum, we erected its palimpsest over the village. Awkward, ungainly, it brinked unbalanced. The roost then populous, the strident morning cry, a bus unloading. It was heralded as a fantastical yet unpopular movement.

At once vaporous and systematic, the urban surface sheathed modes of our most intimate pronouncements. Plugged in, hooked up, in touch, we thought we had intention, yet sensed our intimacies slowly vanishing. Unformulated. Though staged. Our personal turning into personnel, our arias to aerosols, disguises becoming trusted and typical appendages. If we were tactful, we wanted fare. If fed, we were flimsy. If we spread our legs, it was a languorous gesture of tackling distance. On festive days, held infrequently, the populace would gather feed. The city then innocuous to our seduction. Our temptations sprouted weeds, our attempts waxed implausible: an *entracte* entreating acts to mission. One neighbour aspired operatic to distraction, another dolloped the urban with rural habits, a third hung conflicts from the clotheslines in ragged imaginings. In theatres we entered via the backstage, the wings, among the aisles, the floodlights, between the seats we entered into what would become a long, arduous and possibly futile search for the miraculous.

From the public square, the lines shot outwards, prevailed over opposing routes. The lines had been designated, cemented long before our time, and they were likely to outlast us. In their conviction, the lines were resplendent. In their certitude, oppressive. While in the square, among the gas and barricades, the human vines and noisy obstructions, batteries of life kept tempo, and the fable gathered force rising out of inarticulation, inebriated by the violated scenery. Suspicious, the scene beheld us. We resolved to be stoic. We resolved to hold our ground even as it crumbled beneath vulnerable extremities. We wanted to be part of history. Though our history was flimsy. Fabulous. A barricaded fable for which we lacked devices.

Though we knew it to bleed and suffer, suffocate and limp, war remained for the time being a concept, a notion we folded under our arms, took for a stroll, left on the table with the remains of the morning's victuals. War was casual and our casualness embittered us, for war was anything but casual.

We were told that a raft would blossom and we would be salvaged. We were told chronicles, legends and fantastical fictions. Assembled before glowing screens, we were shown spectacles meant to astound us, convince our predecessors, progenies, successors that the tailings of our floundering efforts would have substance. The reliquaries had become kitsch; the temples, fodder for camera-wielding tourists; museums, a way to pass the time in foreign cities; scenic vistas, backdrops for irrelevant human inventions. At times, very rarely, we were troubled by paralyzing questions: this, us, so parasitical? We were told that a raft would be at the ready and we would be salvaged. We were given accounts, reports and statistically supported studies. We were shown spectacles meant to convince us.

Away from the city, journeys proved to be perilous and convoluted. We intimated in different directions, while our connection with the city remained umbilical. As we threaded hand gestures towards the outer regions, we marked. Frontiers, neighbours, systems. Tenuous and fragile. Theoretical and economic. Occasionally, a hopeful dash of yellow flourished.

If our method was to be extraordinary, we needed amplitude, we needed judgment. We wanted ammunition of a different kind. We wanted to be fearless, yet days found us cowering in debilitating apathy. As nodes of being, we still lacked conviction. Though we were methodical, which offered a glimmer of the possible. They avowed our age was transcending its postcolonialist, postliterary, postideological, postindustrialist, posthumanist, postmodernist, postpositivist, postreligious, poststructuralist character, yet everywhere we looked, the posts stood firmly guarded. Delivering at times with haste, at times in nets, by beast or horse, the hunger of our wilful next.

Thresholds

All Aboard!

At dawn, when the ship seemed steady below me, its flamed helm pointing us west, I would take my rare strolls between Cancer and Capricorn, starboard, to watch the peril of my successors set adrift, the way fog might drift. I knew the route of the new Columbus was not through those straits, but the row of sails, wind-swollen, were urging us all on.

I can't trust the sea. (With its foam and convulsive gasps, its hospitality for all creatures save us, breathing heavily on this wooden tub.) I'm not much of a sailor.

One morning, I thought I saw the archipelago, lacy shores of those islands we were all longing for. I raised the alarm. I wanted to be the messenger.

In exchange for a moment of rest, beneath my bare feet the sand catches fire. In the balance of the posthumous flora, we are refused, forbidden from alighting.

I floated away from that silken shore of the first parting from myself.

We've no choice but to continue our journey, though I know I have nothing to offer. I am simply a man with a boat.

Silken Shore

Lake asleep in a dusking leaf, the hair of a peasant I killed awaits to strangle me. Its ridicule on this final step feverishly summoned, the mane's adroitness won't pass down to my successors.

I am a flamed wheel, visible to those who have enemied me for a long while.

Somewhere, in the pleasure of the great distance, a vaporous flag ascends and descends; soldiers bloody their nakedness, hands grasping convulsively; sky, unused to incidents of this kind, blooms too soon.

We can't expect hospitality, though we wear melancholy's gloves. We trench in, we are the despotic fanfare of a blind platoon. We refuse sleep.

Tears march embittered through the snows. We watch them approach, soldier the urge to run off with a shadow, this night on the eve of a new flag.

Blazed

For every veined petal, one by one, soldiers are sent into battle
Ash constellates unspeakably beautiful
Rekindle their eyes
Flames envelop
Foliage incessant
Luminous swarms, torrents, flies so close
To look at the world is submissive
Let's walk among the roses
Roses?
The great Southern Cross refuses to move
Hours pass
There is rustling though no wind
There is a swamp gone back to the blaze
Where the drowned dispute over their crowns of scales
The soldier with his fine fingers shrills, chains, sleeps
Stands a colossal despair
They've found nothing
Frozen lake slowly unfastens its glass doves
When they burst, someone will speak, hinder the advance,
    someone will stand the blaze

The Plank

Separation's wreath over my eyelashes, I would walk the plank. I had awakened in a land of footbridges. My shoulder was scorched. The hour was yesterday's hour and when I parted from you it will be too late.

This is the moment to speak, though I am a face blindfolded. My enormous steps, having enemied me for a long while, clang. The plank repeats the performance of my rambles with greater and greater speed.

I denouement.

You've sent the young catafalque to summon my face, but I cannot balance. Instead I send you my dishevelled hands. Below, in the chambers, they will watch at your living breast our waltz drift off to sleep.

To step on this plank is to step on a threshold. Dusk blooms in the flowering clouds. I think I hear your laugh love.

Signalled

In isolation the explorers will embrace
A messenger, unknown to me, stands on my toes
Watch her approach through the snow
They've drained my strength
Where would I stop if not up there?
The vastness offers hands in exchange for the heightitude of a
  bloody embrace
A creature with apricot-coloured eyes marches off
How does flight begin?
In the fold of a flag?
Soil sprouts a maddened weed at her living breast
A creature with apricot-coloured eyes is no longer useful
Clamour without
A smaller bird mouths your name
Mourning drunk from a glass or mourning drunk from a palm
Do we scorch one another or?
You must believe to be told what awaits
Clamour withholds
As such there is no message

Tightrope Walker

I was Petronius walking the great divide. Mountains near us, below the valley of sorrow.

For every stained petal you extinguished a word. For every stained word you lit the sky with a muted constellation of rain. You were a stifled cry. I bent towards you mother, kissed you, and left.

There were nights when I thought your eyes.

Below, on the green dunes of limestone, people have gathered. They've set out from the desert to empty their sand all around you so you can't take root. Rain falls erratic over the urn fortress, which, submissive, gives up its arms and is filled. Torrents of wine pour down my cheeks.

Dawn is the gash of a silver panther. I am Petronius walking the great divide.

Mirrored

In the glass house who can tell what is mirror or window or
  simply the sash of night?
How it mounts and rambles?
Barefoot with enormous steps
Stairs fall asleep from opiates drunk in a glass
Shadows lag in the sky, turn mad circles, fear the transparency
Will windows clamour what they know?
Do we love one another, or not?
The house is its own enemy
Mirages, splinters glass
Which comrades all forms except the hourglass
Pointing south the house has geography but lacks time
Garden in the midst of a room
Room in the midst of a garden
Acacia dishevelled into sudden fanfare
Plumes plummet
Scrambling up a tree flight begins
No one knows how to billow
A smaller bird gravitates
Your dreaming tongue, exterior wall, blooms too soon

The Bo(a)rders

Sycamores plaster the house's exterior walls. When we would unwittingly open the door and enter, the house's mirrors would bend to collect our shadows. It was before daybreak.

You don your disguise, the peasant's blouse, shadow sewn. Without handrail, the immense stairwell ascends before us. We ascend into the looking glasses, then backtrack and arrive at the step from where we started. A certain coordinate of movements tempts us. We avoid the peril of the windowsill.

In plainer garments you would laugh. We are the spectacular ridicule of black lace on the final step. If we opened the skylight and climbed naked into the sky, the deportations would begin the following day. Rain would fall erratic, waves flood through the windows.

So we climb down a belated ladder through the translucent floor and discharge the rival army, reward it with cities and ports.

On the Threshold

My cheeks spread on the ground
Is it gold? I whisper
Gold
Will they save themselves before daybreak?
In a doorway, a threshold hooded, wearing a vast despair, is
 chained to the sky
When nights begin in the morning, I'll show them the way
You'll welcome them
We'll return upstairs to drown at home, someone will arrive, the
 house will be rented at last
These phosphorescent eyes, these monstrous leaps, who will play?
Trees will thus leaf at a quickened pace
Does daybreak manage to save them?
Your cheeks spread on the threshold stunt a laurel
A human tongue?
Tonight it will rain
From a dead man's mouth
They'll go there barefoot. They'll collide in the dark.
They'll believe in gold.

Borders on Madness

It happened over a game of dice. A die fell through the tombstones. Up in the steeple of the wooden citadel, the bell gonged into a deafening clang.

We challenged the dice, became travellers of mirages.

Time strolled incandescent through its gardens of foliage, swamp and frozen lake: a contagious fire ignited all hours, melting them into a single number. To be its comrade in a new clock, grasping the crush of one night passing.

On the south side of the dial, the train tracks heard the shrill of a locomotive. The air was metallic. Rafael, dragging me after him, hindered by an immense swarm of large, black butterflies, turned: *They alone know the hour! Where is the sky? Where?*

Itinerant Sideline

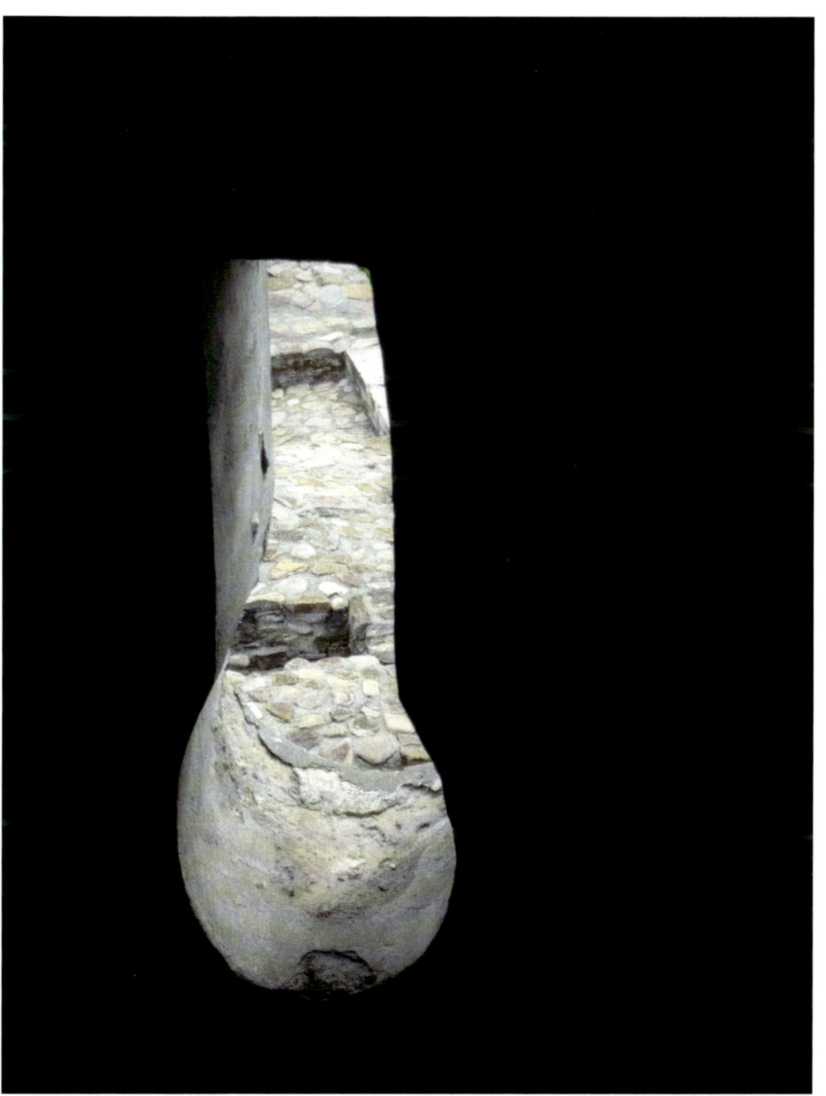

Borne

Si j'écoute, j'écoute avec mes oreilles vampiriques, my empirical mantle, mes sentiments inexistants, mon exactitude. Si j'avale, je dévore, je dévore la brute force de mes sacrements. Aicea aş forţa o margine, le secret sécrète.

Tu énonces un trajet, tu le suis impassiblement, par la suite tu deviens le trajet, deci dacă înţeleg bine, a avea o intenţie commits the already intended. La notion oblique of a drunken following.

Notre constitution nous donne une existence propre à nous. Passage ou contour. We are today all weather wind gusts an ousted leader étendards en flamme copious winged crossings citizen avec citizen, citizen contre citizen, non-citoyenne.

Si j'écoute, j'écoute pour les non-citoyennes. Leur silence qui me rend sourde. En devenant inclassables, elles s'articulent plus fort que cele care se clasifică. They pose the difficult: elles me troublent.

Elle regarde, insouciante et indiscrète, là în ființele où elle existe son existence dangereuse. Flâneurs clignotent advenant comme des étoiles faibles, presque disparues, autour d'elle. Sa fiction se summarize ainsi : cu fiecare zi ce trece, encore une langue s'oublie.

Autrement dit, mon sang-froid te rend mal à l'aise. Mais le réseau te cheamă, te atrage, te attrape.

Vous êtes rivières et rives. În esență riveraine. Born each day, reeds envoilés dans une direction, puis dans l'autre.

Un île qu'il veut défendre, mais les marges s'abîment. Față în față, o resonanță.

Moi, limite, native d'aucune place, d'aucune langue, d'aucun sol natal to call my soul (ce suflet ar putea sufla în mine?), néanmoins les êtres m'utilisent incessamment à travers des ères, me soumettent pour donner forme aux terres, aux espaces, aux idées qu'ils veulent nommer *leurs*. Dans cette langue que j'emprunte, la notion d'*home* ne se manifeste pas.

Acuma, our weathers weep, le contenant ne peut plus nous contenir. Obliterated contentment of containment. Accumulated.

Since to perfectly encounter the limb was not thought possible, tu poursuivais notre rencontre obstinément. Le jour était lourd, portant d'une uneasy faiblesse. The limb, ou le membre si tu veux, was unaccustomed aux fables de ce sort, so in its membrane persisted to pursue its fill, pulsing as though avec une nouvelle vitalité. As such you had to raise the alarm.

Le cheminement de mes propositions s'effrite trop vite : disons que je me mis à nue devant toi, que je me simplifie, que je ne te promettrai plus rien, then I would primate be. Dar totuși politică.

They islanded and shored themselves dans leur collective parlance. L'ère était marquée par les avancements technologiques and linguistic malaise. Complexity donnait place à la vitesse.

Vous me theatricalise. L'infâme bordure du fantasme. Un fanatic se plimbă printre voi.

Élan of elle vers elle par elle prin ea through her à cause d'elle aproape de ea à côté d'elle departe de ea apart from her autour d'elle whereby she frontiers la binding question.

Material matter of utterance, the struggle to persist, lift, take flight, l'angle de la provenance, pointed, aimed, ready to retaliate the retaliation. Le dialogue se rédige en conflit quand on se traduit en *nous* et en *ils*.

The excruciating pleasure of the perhaps. Ponderous and pondering. On dit que tout est médiatisé aujourd'hui. Certes. Mais on articule de petites résistances avec nos organes, antiquate our modernity in a park over a glass.

Si j'éprouve la confusion, je la métamorphose. If I mount, I mind the unease of your citizenship.

Breathing, I come to you, in you. Ton territoire devient le mien. I come as drift, juncture, ouverture dans les parois de ton terrain radical.

Ancillary

Paul Celan's Romanian Poems in Translation

Regăsire

Pe dunele verzi de calcar va ploua astănoapte,
Vinul păstrat până azi într-o gură de mort
Trezi-va ținutul cu punți, strămutat într-un clopot.
O limbă de om va suna într-un coif cutezanța.

Și-așa vor veni într-un pas mai grăbit și copacii,
s-aștepte o frunză cu glas, adusă-ntr-o urnă,
solia coastei de somn trimisă mareei de steaguri.
Scăldată în ochii-ți să fie, să cred că murim împreună.

Părul tău scurs din oglinzi va așterne văzduhul,
în care cu-o mână de ger voi aprinde o toamnă.
Din ape băute de orbi va sui pe o scară târzie
laurul meu scund, ca să-ți muște din frunte.

Regain

Tonight it will rain on the green dunes of limestone.
Wine preserved until now in a dead man's mouth
will awaken the realm of footbridges, displaced in a bell.
A human tongue will clang courage inside a helmet.

And so trees will come at a quickened pace,
to wait for a voiced leaf, brought in an urn,
herald of sleep's coast sent off to a tide of flags.
Let it soak in your eyes, so I think we're dying together.

Your hair streaming from mirrors will blanket the sky
in which, with a frigid hand, I'll flame an autumn.
From waters drunk by the blind, my stunted laurel
will climb a belated ladder to bite from your brow.

Love Song

When for you nights begin at dawn,
our phosphorescent eyes will scurry out of the walls, rattling walnuts,
you'll play with them and a wave will flood the window,
our one shipwreck, the translucent floor through which we'll peer
at the vacant room below our own,
you'll furnish it with your walnuts and curtain the casement with
    your tresses,
someone will come and it will, at last, be rented,
we'll return upstairs to drown at home

Last Night

From trees sown by twilight in our incendiary rooms
we'll slowly unfasten glass doves, foliage incessantly
rustling, they'll sprout on our shoulders and arms, no wind
but a shadowed swamp it will be, where you can't take root,
a frozen lake where the drowned dispute over their crown of scales
and life is a boat ashore, abandoned by oars.
Towards us, a voice will come from the flames to stain its silver in
 blood,
and gone back to the blaze, announce: Not I, but they alone know
 the hour!
Then they'll set out from the desert to empty their sand all around
 you:
let there be mountains near us, let us stay in the Valley of Sorrow—
and you'll slowly unfasten the glass doves, one by one,
and when they burst in the air, you'll speak to me wildly.

Poem for Mariana's Shadow

Love's mint grown like an angel's finger.

You must believe: from the soil sprouts an arm twisted by silences,
a shoulder scorched by the blaze of smothered lights
a face blindfolded with the black sash of sight
a large leaded wing and a leafed one
a body wearied by rest soaked in waters.

Look how it floats amid the grasses with outstretched wings,
how it mounts the mistletoe stairs towards a glass house,
in which, with enormous steps, rambles an aimless seaweed.

You must believe this is the moment to speak to me through the tears,
to go there barefoot, be told what awaits us:
mourning drunk from a glass or mourning drunk from a palm—
and the maddened weed falling asleep hearing your answer.

Colliding in the dark the house's windows will clamour
telling each other what they know, but without discovering
whether we love one another or not.

New Year's Eve

The night of the new year, hourless season,
you sent the young catafalque to summon your lover;
tears marched towards her from the looking glasses, incensed
in the embittered snowed-over taper, risen from a temple.
The ring, snuffed out in a goblet, scrambled to the window
to watch her approach through the snows with her slumbering hair;
dishevelled hands set off to wait for her at the gate,
and above in the chambers came the poets to waltz.
But she trod over the threshold to confront an eyelid,
watch at her living breast a creature drift off to sleep . . .

A die fell between the slabs, with apricot-coloured eyes,
and the steeple of the wooden citadel ran off with a shadow.

Sadness

Dreams, gusts of evening's aurora
lake asleep in a dusking lily,
come freeze them with silences, dark
sister to him who wreathed

your temple with the snow-toothed sky,
hoist on an eyelash the flowering cloud,
adrift in plainer garments, you
laugh: tomorrow, an autumn from walnuts?

The peasant's blouse, shadow-sewn, you refuse,
with the star-impaled spider, to blanket the night . . .
Once more gold sleeps and the fog drifts.
To whom do I give the dew? To whom—the tear?

fragment from an unfinished poem

Your eyes' grasses, bitter grass.
Wind tremors above, the wax eyelid.

Your eyes' waters, forgiven water.

Blinded by monstrous leaps, we, travellers of mirages, met in
renunciation's one single kiss.
The hour was yesterday's hour, a third hand pointing to it,
incandescent,
which I'd never seen in time's gardens—
the other two ail embracing on the south side of the dial.

When they'll part it will be too late, time will be another, the foreign
hand will turn mad circles igniting all hours with a contagious fire
and melting them into a single number
which at the same time will be the hour, season and the twenty-four
steps I'll take the instant I die
then it will jump through the splintered glass into the middle of the
room
invite me to follow, be its comrade in a new clock that will measure
a time much larger.

I for one prefer that time be measured with the hourglass,
so it be a finer time, as your hair's shadow in the sand, so I could
trace its contour with blood, grasping that one night has passed.
I for one prefer the hourglass, so you could crush it when I tell you
eternity's lie.

I prefer it as you prefer the serpents to my hair of uncertain
shimmers,
I prefer the hourglass because I can smash it easily with grief's cane
compelling a large wing born in autumn to lag in the sky, which in
the time I sleep next to you, shifts colour.

Lacking a handrail, the immense stairwell, where the vaporous flag of encountering your own self ascends and descends, remains the single certain coordinate of movements that tempt me still. Though lacking a handrail, I accept them, even prefer them, for my rare strolls between Cancer and Capricorn, when, squabbling with the season, I flood the house with the black lace of a pleasure to love no one. Just as rare, though beneath an interior sky signalled by a baton, I, a flamed wheel at the far edge of the steps, descend to the very bottom, where the hair of a woman I killed awaits to strangle me. I avoid the peril with an adroitness that won't pass down to my successors. Then backtrack to arrive at the initial step and repeat the performance with greater and greater speed, until the spectacular ridicule of the mane on the final step. Now—and only now!—am I visible to those who, having enemied me for a long time, wait feverishly for the denouement. But, unused to incidences of this kind, they think me the iron handrail of the stairwell and, unaware of the danger, descend to the bottom to unwittingly open the door through which the Defunct Illustrious will make her entrance.

The deportations set to begin the following day, at night came Rafael, hooded, wearing a vast despair of black silk, his burning gaze cross-eyed on my brow, torrents of wine began pouring down my cheeks, spread on the ground, people sipped them asleep.—Come, said Rafael, draping over my overly luminous shoulders a despair similar to the one he carried. I bent towards mother, kissed her incestuously, and left the house. An immense swarm of large, black butterflies, come from the tropics, hindered my advance. Rafael dragged me after him and we went down towards the train tracks. Beneath my feet I felt the rails, heard the shrill of a locomotive, fervently close, my heart clamped up. The train trailed above our heads.

I opened my eyes. Facing me, across an extensive expanse, stood a colossal candelabrum with thousands of arms.—Is it gold?! I whispered to Rafael.—Gold. You'll climb on one of its arms, so when I have raised it into the vault you can chain it to the sky. Before daybreak, people will manage to save themselves, flying towards it. I'll show them the way, you'll welcome them.

I climbed on one arm, Rafael passed from one arm to the next, touching each in turn, the candelabrum began to rise. A leaf settled on my brow, the same spot my friend's gaze had grazed, a maple leaf. I glance around me: this can't be the sky. Hours pass and I've found nothing. I know: below people gathered, Rafael grazed them with his fine fingers, they rose, and I still haven't stopped.

Where is the sky? Where?

Maybe one day, when the rehabilitation of the solstices becomes official, compelled by the atrocity with which people will skirmish with the trees of the great azure boulevards, maybe that same day you'll kill yourselves, all four at once, tattooing death's hour in the budding skin of your Spanish dancer brows, tattooing this hour with the still timid yet no less venomous arrows of an adios' adolescence.

Maybe I'll be nearby, maybe you'll have warned me of the great event and I'll face you when your eyes, descended to the distant chambers of the conservatory, where, while alive, obliged by no one, you exiled yourselves to contemplate the eternal immobility of the boreal palm trees, when your eyes will expose the world to the undying beauty of the somnambulist tigers . . . Maybe then I'll find the courage to contradict you, the instant when, after so much fruitless waiting, we'll have found a common tongue. Depends on you, if I stir, with fingers spread fanlike, the faintly salted breeze of the requiem for victims of an end's first rehearsal. On you too depends if I descend my handkerchief into your mouths devastated by the fire of the false prophecies, then go flaunting it in the street above the concrescent heads of the multitudes as they gather near the city's one fountain to focus into its depths, one by one, on the last drop of water; I'll flaunt it incessantly, silent and with gestures that forbid any other message.

Depends on you. Believe me.

Once more I suspended great white parasols from the night's vault. I know, the route of the new Columbus is not through here, my archipelago will remain undiscovered. The endless ramifications of the aerial roots, from which I hung many a hand, will embrace in isolation, unknown to the explorers of heightitude, the hands will grasp convulsively and never cast off melancholy's gloves. All this I know, just as I know I can't trust the tides, which, with a foam as from the deep, bathe the lacy shores of those islands I long for with their despotic sleep. Beneath my bare feet the sand catches fire. I stand on the tips of my toes and raise myself up there. I don't expect hospitality, I also know this, but where would I stop if not there? I'm not welcomed. An unfamiliar messenger meets me at large to announce that I am forbidden from alighting anywhere. I offer my hands bloodied by the floating thorns of the nocturnal sky in exchange for a moment of rest, hoping that from there, that silken shore of the first parting from myself, I'll be able to raise a row of circular, wind-swollen sails, and continue my course towards him. I offer my hands to watch over the equilibrium of this posthumous flora, keep it out of all peril. Once more I'm refused. No choice but to continue my course, though they've drained my strength and I shut my eyes to search for a man with a boat.

It seems believable that all they said about the acacia cross is enough to forbid your leave. You drained light's beginnings from the mirror, you indulged intoning the acrostic of the unsullied traveller in scents, sullen and clairvoyant like onion flower, you sighed seeing kerchiefs shaken in gardens, you summoned Mariana, summoned her with a colour squandered along with life's inks, but you forgot that a chamber is not a chestnut, that its foliage is eaten with memory's spoon and that the south-facing doors are keyless. You could've crossed their thresholds before dawn flooded engulfed by embalmed surges, to flood with the lakes surging from the walls, leap with the snowballs forgotten in the eyes of anthropophagous shrubs, to say again—the last time—the word hanging from the translucent icon of your indefatigable throat: *rust*. Rusted was the barren where you ventured with your sandal contaminated by the poetry of your paper adolescence, rusted was the adolescent paper you stepped over to reach the threshold. So you gave up.

You decided to climb the acacia without exerting the precarious effort of the star diviner. The stars . . . How often you wanted to remember their fulgurant eclipse in the honey set out on the table of poisons . . . It was the sort of exercise that made you leave the city. You left in daylight, when everyone could see you, suitcase crammed in the brain, pencil spread out above the wax amalgam and the first quarter moon.

How joyous it was to scatter murmurful goblets on the hexagonal slabs of love. No one saw you. Alone you scoured the streets shielded by enormous parasols, parachutes of dwarfs run again into the ground. The air dinned, a din of celibate coins come to see you depart. For a moment you stopped to look at them, your coat unbuttoned: how else to satisfy your chest's lacy curiosity if not so? You were told of lairs and blackbirds. Stubborn and impassioned by the allogeneic extremities of strolling, you thought it was time to find them, despite the frozen inheritances. Once again, you were misled.

Couldn't you see that your steps led towards feathered monotonies? That the vast chamber of possibility imperilled by ringed falcons no longer corresponded to the flag staked in the marsh with people disguised as motorboats? Couldn't you understand that to be a traveller imposed the leprous curtain of bloody tents? Ah, no one inside the tent? The rival's raven perched on the coat of arms above its entrance? The rival's raven, his hair tea-yellowed by the light of the birdless hour? Were you asked for a monosyllabic courageous act? A jaunt through the pillaged scenery of impulses analogous to the poppy? Yes, it's tough to find a place where the sand pampered by coal hands is kept. It's tough to bear the orphan dreams of mourning orbits. It's tough . . .

But tell me, you who could flutter your lustrous atrocities, the glaring of one obsessed by rest stops glutted with the toothed tadpoles of leafless tidings, you, messenger of abscissas blossomed in tear salt—answer me:

Who was the first to drown? Who ran down the stairs with dishevelled hair and hardened the uneven undulations of posterity? Who ran out of a lover's breast on a horse stolen from the neighbours? Who dodged the cloak, was . . . [*here the text breaks off; the next page is missing*]

It's come, at last, the moment when, facing the mirrors that plaster the house's exterior walls where you abandoned your lover forever dishevelled, you hoist your black flag to the top of the acacia, bloomed too soon. Sharply, you hear the fanfare of the blind platoon, the last to be loyal to you, you don your disguise, fasten black lace to the sleeves of your ashen costume, scramble up the tree, the flag's folds envelop you, flight begins. No, no one knows how to billow like you around this house. Night falls, you float on your back, the house's mirrors constantly bend to collect your shadow, stars plummet to shear your disguise, your eyes drain heartwards, where the sycamore has enflamed its leaves, the stars descend there too, all till the very last, a smaller bird, death, gravitates around you and your dreaming tongue mouths your name.

Partisan of erotic absolutism, reticent megalomaniac even among divers and simultaneous messenger of the halo Paul Celan, I won't evoke the petrifying physiognomy of the aerial shipwreck except once a decade (or more) and won't skate, except at a late hour, on a lake guarded by the colossal forest of the acephalous members of the Universal Poetic Conspiracy. It's easy to see that here the arrows of visible fire won't penetrate. An immense curtain of amethyst dissembles beyond the forest outskirts the existence of this anthropomorphic vegetation from which I attempt, selenic, a dance to astonish me. I've yet to succeed and, with eyes moved to the temples, look at myself in profile, waiting for spring.

There were nights when I thought your eyes, under which I drew dark orange circles, were rekindling their ash. Those nights, rain fell erratic. I'd open the windows and climb naked on the windowsill to look at the world. From the forest, trees marched towards me, one by one, submissive, a defeated army laying down their arms. I'd stay still as the sky lowered the flag by which it had sent its soldiers into battle. From a recess you'd watch me sitting there, unspeakably beautiful in my bloody nakedness: I was the only constellation the rain hadn't extinguished, I was the great Southern Cross. Yes, those nights it was hard to open your veins when the flames enveloped me, the urn fortress was mine, I'd fill it with my blood after discharging the rival army, rewarding it with cities and ports, while the silver panther gashed at the dawn shadowing me. I was Petronius, once more spilling my blood among the roses. For every stained petal you extinguished a torch.

Remember? I was Petronius and I didn't love you.

Riverine

Le langage est notre premier exil.

Ion Caraion

1. *Overpass*

PC: . . . with what words, with what silence?

NS: The ice melted.

PC: All the unanswerable questions in these dark days.
This ghostly mute not-yet.

NS: Then you came with the holy word.

OA: We begin, always, in the dark. A dim, rough cabin forested on the frontier, at the crux of a mountain pass. Await night to cross.

OA: The lake is unfeasible. So too the river. The sky taut.

OA: Her countenance betrays signs of distress, even panic. I say my goodbyes, not having the faintest idea of what it means. We leave by car, truck, bus, on foot, by plane, by inflatable boat, by train. Decades pass. Have we arrived?

OA: Recurrent invention of the ex_______.

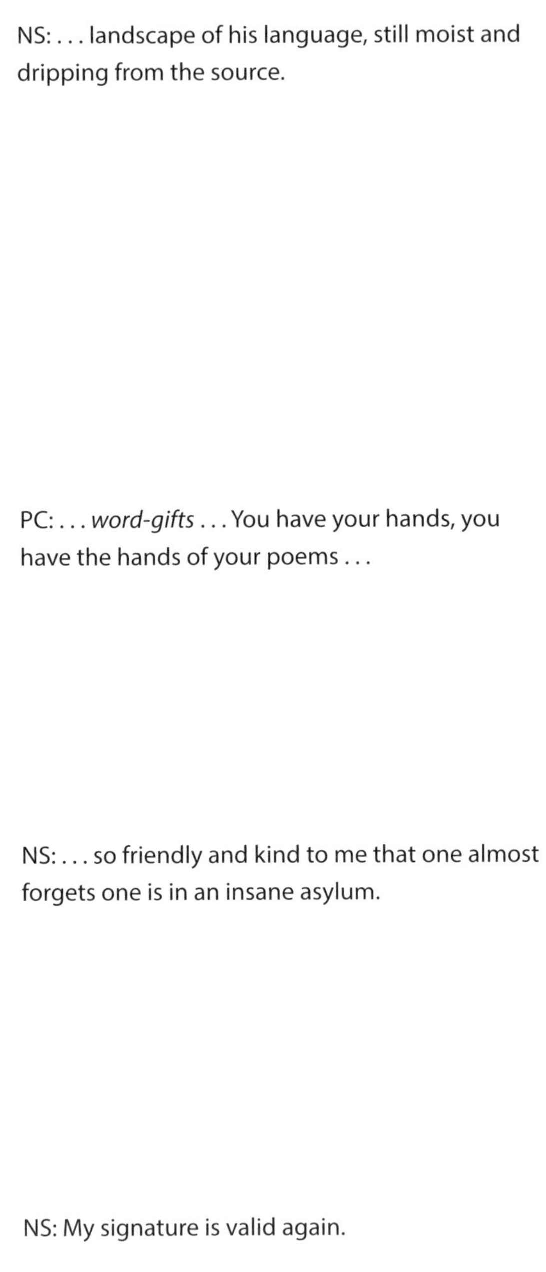

NS: . . . landscape of his language, still moist and dripping from the source.

PC: . . . *word-gifts* . . . You have your hands, you have the hands of your poems . . .

NS: . . . so friendly and kind to me that one almost forgets one is in an insane asylum.

NS: My signature is valid again.

OA: We cross into the literal "out of doors" of foreign, its Latin forest. Travel, vulnerable and clumsy, to the new species-city. Enter its orb. We are not special, not political. The city constellates through us with its intersecting entities. The city noisy, invisible, dying, groping, flourishing and extravagant. With time, outside its doors, inside the elements, we harden.

OA: Language besets us: a parapet at first, then a colonizing sea, eventually a recognizable landscape. Its weather balmy and volatile.

OA: The insanity is a necessity. We have to pass through. The asylum will be or will not be waiting for us on the other side. Which, before we know it, has become our side. Which, before we know it, has given meaning to "sides."

NS: It has been black for us both for so long, I felt for you through countries.

PC: . . . thank you for your lines, for the reminder of that light.

OA: On one side, I practise signing the name from the old country until its signature becomes. On the other, I mime. The sign of away.

OA: Through the countries, tongues murmuring, glimmering. Not silent, even when cut off.

My river is the language in which
foreign language, obsolete rickety
estranged. Sometimes strangled.

Or the river's bowels to be dredged. Or m
violence to be resisted. Yet the assigning
affection to bestow upon the river, rather

Meanwhile the
displacement,
manqué in the

He had called it *ținutul cu punți* anticipating that French city with
river of thirty-seven bridges where he would come to dwell. When
land, I saw a *realm of footbridges* transposing my francophone dw
ligament of language aqueducts. I was almost thirty-seven when
this thinking. He was just twenty-seven when crossing frontiers to
French tributary.

Strămutat într-un clopot, he and I were. O
would later invent it. Melodious and deaf
Disjunctive and disorienting the new ton
composing a resonance. In this *there*, wh

et. My familial language, his first
planks to be crossed and re-crossed,

s surface to will. As such. A
already a first violence. Or an
an articulation of belonging.

embrace of the urban island occupies, causes the
f my own, I will not call it exile (though at times a bit
buoyancy).

ulating
s saw
into a
ed into
by the

ced in a bell as my English
were the new sounds.
et exerting an undeniable pull,
ame a *here*, in the new alien

langue, appropriated though not maternal,
continents, in our varied centuries, sought

A tour
mass g
swells

The logical forms of his river and mi
river and mine are separate. Or the
distinct worlds for they are decades
mine are unfixed yet continuous, al
towards the same ocean. Which is r
on *țărmul de mătase al primei despă*
opposite *silken shore of the first par*
the first river. The child self, disconti

Pitching the intimate tongues against the public language, the rive
or flourish. Though he saw his life as *barca la mal, părăsită de vâsl*
boat ashore, abandoned by oars, he willed words into oars. Or word
transformed into wounds. Until a body and a river met. A failing of
Or a matter, always, of a prolonged submersion?

Who was the first to drown?
întâi? My river courses with
mixed, a mongrel. *Qui se no*
ecosystem.

eparately, on our different
ɔssibility of a kind of freedom.

:e wedging the continent, a provocateur, bold before the oceanic
g on its mouth, bold in its commerce of provocation, my river
spring. The runoff of knowledge.

different. Or the logical forms of his
forms of his river and mine exist in
Or the logical forms of his river and
as they flow on their two continents
same. Disjointed by time, he stands
e mine. Momentarily, I stand on the
ɔm myself. Self of the first language,

n lush
he
ɔeen
ge?

ver asks no such questions. *Care s-a înecat*
:kish water, its tides and sediments, impure,
emier? My river is suspect. And its own

Rarely is the river silent, though my brut bruit thre
inaction, egregious. The meridian still a far-off wis

Țărmurile dantelate ale insulelor acestora pe care le vreau became
those islands I longed for, cells not a state but stated, water swilli
rocks, trees winded and whooshed, while a freight train rumble
no longer signalling terror. Quieted, a language struggles not to

In the grammar of dawn, not a hint of irony. The intricacies of
compel me. *Unde e cerul?* he kept asking, looking up, *unde?* Lo
panic: where is the sky?

My river encloses the city. His divides it. A
evokes a frigid winter sky painted in an ur
months, the river balances.

Nu mă pot încrede în mare
nedescoperit, he endured
which bathe so *my archip*

Because the island is itself an archipelago of eras, use and
catches fire across the water. Its destructive splendour gl
awhir with traffic, while rapids fluster and crickets pitch t
bold as precipice and passage. And I grasp, at last, *naufra*
aerial shipwreck.

The brut bruit of
river glints.

ores of
inst
distance,
ler.

erness
up, I

t to conjugate the bridge
ingly crystalline blue. For

scaldă so *arhipelagul meu va rămâne*
multitudes confluence. *I can't trust the tides*
will remain undiscovered, I bear.

e, history
the urban sky
gh in the river
erian in the

3. *Current*

— But isn't that . . . the signature?

— The signature. When your locality enveloped mine.

— When my locality breathed yours, your limbs were already longing for the blade.

— Thus the terror in the river, read over and over again. Floundering the bounty.

— The cinders also. So many fittings. I could not know them, not sincerely, not well. Though the decay chafed at my chest, entrails, gullet.

4. *Overflow*

— But isn't that the bold open maw of your wish to comprehend, meaning to devour?

— The chewing, when I wallowed, growing a green film of grime, a swelter of flies, a stagnant pool with no way in and no way out.

— When the stagnation peaked, there stood still more stagnation. Then the pen broke, the screen faltered, the tongue came loose, a random organ flopped and floundered like a fish out of water.

— So the flood made good on its threat through pipes, tunnels, heat vents and air ducts, subway conduits, sewer channels, wells, reservoirs, basements and crypts, fissuring the city, replacing its grid with a forgotten tangle of old springs and streams.

— The labyrinth breached. The breathing oven, this apparatus for my longing. Right then, the scaffolds scaled the building and stayed through winter.

— The decay of the West and the South . . .

— To pasture in. Is resonance the wind's passing lance, its abeyance, or the wind's depth? Word branches resemble one another. Fits of dismantlement, ravings.

— Everysediment and inference.

— The inference and no-sediment.

— To pasture in: to vouch for the afflicted.

— And margins? Vouch for them also. Margins hound margins.

— I was in a hallway, in Paris, when the river's prose rammed the threshold: a rush, a blaring of lashings.

— At times: the river's prose. At times: no-sediment. Inference and what the island adheres.

— And what the island adheres: storms to privations.

— The decay of the steady and the firm could be read daily in the newspapers.

— And when the waters receded, still the scaffolding remained. By then, without their spines, the building would collapse.

— And sediments. Leftovers from the other tongue.

— Tossed and turned, refused to settle.

— To weather this, to come through, marked, rusted, grimy, sopping, feverish, yet to come through.

— And outcasts? Their tongues too, split, dry, left hanging. Having to learn the day's new idiom, its weather.

— I was in a tenement, in another island city, when the sea rose to meet the river at full force.

— At once: the sea rose. At once: leftovers from the other tongue. Sediments and what our islands withstand.

— And what our islands withstand: tempests made intimate on tongues.

— Or vegetation to the depths.

— Vegetation to the depths? Trigger it and nurture it.

— Depth of our textual inklings.

— Uttering the signature of watercourses.

— Or any destitution of interior.

— The crevice: is this instigation?

— A generative crevice.

— The electric indigo of dusk.

— The furrow on a brow? Release it and let it flow.

— The assembling and disassembling of the species-city.

— Groping the vagrancies of aqueous soundings.

— Or any decimation of exterior.

— The city: is it syllabic?

— An urb-species.

5. *Suspension / Sediment*

The girl comes to the river. Kicks a rock with the toe of one foot. A leaf drifts in. The current is anxiously. The girl comes and sits on a rock down by the river. A grey-glass day, a day of loose gravel. The wind blows a wisp of hair into her eyes. Intermittently. The girl pushes the wisp out of her eyes. Intermittently. The eyes are dark brown polished glass. The river drifts sediments of loose gravel, live kick of fidgety fish. Syllables unlock the. Mesh of wind gusts. By the river, a girl drifts, sifting a day of pebbles through the mesh of her fingers in her left pocket. The pebbles are syllables leftover from the other language. A haunting, a forest hut, a legend. Or a map of the river. Unfolded. Its gusty roads. Babbled over by fish. Current and torrential. In the girl's hand, the rough cut of stone hurts. Intermittently.

The river holds the girl in its folds. Eddies and wet and slime between the toes, the green tang of rot. The folds many and moving as if propelled by thousands of arms. The girl folded in the middle. A partly opened book. Or one closing. The girl, a book, not blank but folding. In the surging river held fast to the sky by a sudden downpour. The river and the pouring sky. Sky and the thrashing river. The girl intermittently. Green eddies of rot infiltrating between her toes, slithering as if penned in a fold. Thousand-pebbled serpent on the skin's page. Paper and pulp and the rot of sky. Sudden surge. Day held fast to her fold. The girl, intermittent, opening, closing. Her odour, her tongue.

A bridge over the river like a scar. The girl on the bridge, a red welt. Hungry, the bridge over the river like a discordant chord, a stray musical staff. Over and the girl on the bridge. Still. Discerning the horizon from. Rapids from mists. Melodious discord of. The girl's voice scarring the setting. River welling with sun. With whitewater. With a girl and her thirsty palate. Taste of her cheeks in the mist, of the river in her mouth, of the welt on the bridge. A hunger, a welling and a stray musical staff. And a bridge waiting for the river to devour it. Through the mists stillness holds. And the girl's mouth deafening.

A girl with the old continent beneath tremoring in the current. Contingent on her tremor of away, the girl with the old current bound. Drift of pale green. Glutted. A half-sunken boat as a nostalgic gesture. Cracked verdant mud. On the disused steps, a ritual mapping. Sunken and glutted the pale-green drift of her continent. As days skip rocks in the current, make faint ripples, then sink. Shifting, a continent chained. To restless wind stammer. Caught in the drift. A girl. As though contingent upon a nostalgic gesture.

Inbound and clamorous, the calamity of. An invasion on the river, struggling in vain to shift its flow, yet bound to its eternal east. The girl reduced to a stammer, a babble. Tension of disquiet torrential in the current. Bound veins of contingent weeds. Afterthoughts of extremities. Extraneous ellipses. The girl trying to form an island of stillness, if only as a formulation of the mind. Intense stammers, disgorged, redacted. The girl stubbornly silent, stubbornly solitary.

The river flowing, gushing, swelling, evaporating, the river running off, arriving, the river simply and the girl absent. A blinding sky reflecting in the river. The stones and river grasses also. And the girl not. Boats and tugboats and the ghostly port, the defunct cranes and rusted weed-entangled rail tracks, the distant mayhem of an amusement park, the whooshing, sloshing gurgle of water, echo of a distant long-forgotten conflict, the industry of wheat, lumber and coal corroded to a trade of tourists, an intermittent circus. And the girl away. Sunday strollers swelling on the artificial beach, cameras digitizing frozen smiles, strident screams, heels murmuring on pavement, a promise of amusement in the former warehouses, generic pop beats of the café with a view. And the girl gone.

Boats on the river marking stresses of linguistic fluency. Pauses and vowellings, intoned, tuned, striated. Hawked, caught in the throat. The girl, truant, watches the river. Populated. Mouths herself into an allegory of the river's markings.

The river with a girl in its wake. Or a wakeful city. Or a girl being a city. The river's frozen edges and rushing core. The river carrying winter on its back. The girl carrying wind on hers. While the obscene beauty of the other watercourse carries her, constantly, into the expanse. Or the exhilaration. A juncture or passage laboriously inserts itself into the pact. Between girl and river. A train tacked onto a riverbank labours through rock, hail, valleys, wind, joins and dismembers the cardinal points of the compass. Words empty, spill out, like upturned vessels.

Peripheries

The route of the book, an entreaty I could not
ignore. The spoken and the nonspoken, dense
markings of the calling

Because we could speak or not, we sometimes
chose not to utter, even if only silence was
withheld

Because the wind tried to rattle submission into
the leaves, I bore lust in my abdomen

Because a yellow stain in our field of vision is an
intimate pronouncement

Because later our fantasies would famish our
today

Because the day basked more extravagantly after

Because an opulent tongue contours my hip
bone

Because the music arrived in ochres, greens,
yellows

Because I wanted the music to articulate me

Because lacking ardour, the surroundings were
impoverished

Because I am a pronoun in disguise as sediment

Because fleshy, abundant, undulating, the river
revelled in the fluid silt of its constancy

Because my hands were sexed and dripping

Because the colour would not contain but hum

Because intricate with lust, the tongue too was
extravagant

Because in pronouncing *aqueous*, I became
aqueous

Because language adhered to the current's
sinuous ligaments, I faced silence

Because the trees bore parasitic beehives of ivy,
they exposed laden vulnerabilities and thus were
known to us

Because the marginals were contingent upon the
marginalized

Because the note held a vigorous few minutes

Because we strapped novel concepts onto our
mounds like erect appendages

Because we were not content with simulacra,
though we revelled in role play

Because I wanted to make want a generous
gesture

Because the chords beckoned yet I mired in
habitual motions

Because our torsos resisted rituals

Because tidal, swelling, littoral tongues meander
over the volatile landscapes altering riverbeds

Because the ebb and flow foliates lavishment

Because displaced yet roseate in the dense
markings

"Ancillary" Annotations

Paul Celan (1920–1970) wrote the sixteen poems, fragments and prose-poems translated in "Ancillary" while living in București, România between 1945 and 1947. These are the only poems that he would ever write in Romanian. Born to German-Jewish parents in Chernivtsi (or Cernăuți or Chernovitsy or Chernovitz)—a city located in Romania at the time but in Ukraine today, whose name has fluctuated numerous times over the centuries depending on its rulers—Paul Pessach Antschel became Paul Celan during his years in Bucharest, having first attempted to translate himself into Paul Aurel and Paul Ancel. Written in one of his adopted languages, in the desolation of the war, a war he survived in a Romanian labour camp while his family died in another, these poems are thresholds, existent and impossible, invented and possible. Limbs disarticulate and wander their syntax in the estranged language, lose control of their articulations, stir in the aftermath of an inhumane civilization. Flags or trees are on the march and the private stands exposed and vulnerable in a transparent house or is at sea looking for a new shore. Time has been made other or bloodied or it has always been incomprehensible. Wordhands are denied rest.

Bookish Limbs

Declining America, Rob Budde
Romanian Poems of Paul Celan
Suis Je/ Plus Je, Hélène Cixous
Dwell, Jeff Derksen
Conference, Stacy Doris
City Gates, Elias Khoury (tr. Paula Haydar)

La maison à penser de P., Suzanne Leblanc
Fable, Robert Pinget
Théorie des prépositions, Claude Royet-Journoud

Responsibility & Judgment, Hannah Arendt
Atlas of Transformation, eds. Zbyněk Baladrán & Vít Harránek
Le Pli, Gilles Deleuze
Adorno's Noise, Carla Harryman
Translating Tradition, Paul Celan in France, ed. Benjamin Hollander
Europeana, Une brève histoire du XXe siècle, Patrik Ourednik (tr. Marianne Canavaggio)
Paul Celan: Dimensiunea românească, Petre Solomon

Acknowledging Notes

The epigraph in "Riverine" is from Ion Caraion, "Les Mots en Exil," in *Marges et Exils* (Brussels: Editions Labor, 1987), 47.

The Paul Celan and Nelly Sachs quotes in "Overpass" are taken from Paul Celan and Nelly Sachs, *Correspondence* (Riverdale-on-Hudson: Sheep Meadow Press, 1995), 7, 10, 13, 16, 36, 40, 42, 63.

The Romanian fragments in "Coursing Vernaculars" come from Paul Celan's Romanian poems.

"Current" and "Overflow" are dialogic transcriptions between the O and the Part exceeded from Jean Daive's conversant walk with Paul Celan, which Daive transmuted into the Other and the Patriarch in his *Jeu des séries scéniques* in *Translating Tradition* (San Francisco: Acts: A Journal of New Writing, 1988). The syntax was lifted. Then spilled over.

Versions of some poems have previously appeared in *Aufgabe*, *The Capilano Review*, *Corresponding Voices*, *CV2*, *Dandelion*, *Poetry Is Dead*, *Hilda*, *ooteoote* and *Truck*. Thank you to the editors.

Some of the work was imagined or written while a writer in residence at the University of Calgary (Calgary Canadian Writer in Residence, 2010–2011) and at CAMAC (France, 2014), and while frequently crossing the border between New York and Montreal. Thank you for the generous support, luxury of time and provocation.

Thank you to the Estate of Paul Celan and to Suhrkamp Verlag for permission to re-envision Paul Celan's Romanian poems in English, and to the Conseil des arts et des lettres du Québec and the Canada Council for the Arts for travel support.

Thank you to Erín Moure for editing acumen and constant encouragement, Fred Wah and Lyn Hejinian for joyous support, Garry Thomas Morse for the initial publishing enthusiasm, and Stephen Collis, Greg Gibson, Kevin Williams and the Talonbooks team for their hard work and belief in this book.

A very special thank-you to Pam Dick for everything.

Limbinal is for P.D. and P.C., without whom these word worlds would not be possible.

© 2015 Oana Avasilichioaei

All rights reserved. No part of this book may be reproduced, stored in a retrieval system, or transmitted, in any form or by any means, without the prior written consent of the publisher or a licence from Access Copyright (the Canadian Copyright Licensing Agency). For a copyright licence, visit accesscopyright.ca or call toll free to 1-800-893-5777.

Paul Celan poems: All rights reserved by and controlled through Suhrkamp Verlag Berlin.

Talonbooks
278 East First Avenue, Vancouver, British Columbia, Canada V5T 1A6
www.talonbooks.com

First printing: 2015

Typeset in Myriad
Printed and bound in Canada

Interior design by Oana Avasilichioaei
Typesetting and cover design by Typesmith
Cover and interior photographs by Oana Avasilichioaei

Talonbooks gratefully acknowledges the financial support of the Canada Council for the Arts, the Government of Canada through the Canada Book Fund, and the Province of British Columbia through the British Columbia Arts Council and the Book Publishing Tax Credit.

Library and Archives Canada Cataloguing in Publication

Avasilichioaei, Oana, author
Limbinal / Oana Avasilichioaei.

Poems.
Includes sixteen poems by Paul Celan translated from Romanian into English by the author.
ISBN 978-0-88922-924-2 (pbk.)

1. Celan, Paul—Translations into English. I. Title.

PS8551.V38L54 2015 C811'.6 C2014-907070-5

Poetry by Oana Avasilichioaei

We, Beasts
Expeditions of a Chimæra (with Erín Moure)
feria: a poempark
Abandon

Translations by Oana Avasilichioaei

The Thought House of Philippa, Suzanne Leblanc (with Ingrid Pam Dick)
Universal Bureau of Copyrights, Bertrand Laverdure
Wigrum, Daniel Canty
The Islands, Louise Cotnoir
Occupational Sickness, Nichita Stănescu